Love, Quarantined
Written by Tommy Watkins

I sit alone in my house, wishing you were here.
Waiting and waiting for a text to come.

Days and Days, still nothing has come. Looking outside, I see the clouds. It's us holding each other.

Dancing with each other, we laugh happily. We a

in love.

Looked back at my phone, still nothing. No call, no text, nothing. I get mad! How could this be happening? Even before this quarantine began, I suppose we grew apart.

But I fell in love with you, isn't that enough? Wh[y]
don't you respond to me?

You didn't want to go deeper into our relationship because of our situation, but don't you love me?

My phone is on low battery, and still no text or call. I feel alone in my head. Is it me? Am I a loser? Are you with another man? Do you love him

32

I click on social media on my phone, and I see it.
You do love him. You are even engaged to him.

I sit on the floor, not going how to act. I though
we would get married and have a family.

I wipe my tears and get up. I can't live like this. I need to change my life! Something new, something different, something that will make me believe in myself again!

I get up and start a new day. This day is full of hope and belief in me. I look outside, and the sun is shining. Today is my beginning.

The End